IMAGES
of America

FRANKLIN

David Demaree Banta, seen in this late-1880s portrait, was an early historian in Johnson County. He was born in Franklin in 1833 and educated in the local schools and at Franklin College. He later entered Indiana University and earned a degree in law. He practiced law in Franklin and later became a circuit court judge before retiring from the court to become dean of the School of Law at Indiana University from 1889 until his death in 1896. A prolific history author, he is best known for his 1881 *Historical Sketch of Johnson County*. (Johnson County Museum of History.)

ON THE COVER: Automobiles were still rather rudimentary "horseless carriages" when this group of Franklin High School Bicycle Club members posed for a photograph in front of a popular local bicycle retailer in 1900. Bicycles were not only used for recreation and sport, but they also served as popular transportation vehicles for much of the Franklin population at the beginning of the 20th century. (Johnson County Museum of History.)

IMAGES
of America

FRANKLIN

Jim Hillman and John Murphy
with the Johnson County Museum of History

ARCADIA
PUBLISHING

Published by Arcadia Publishing
Charleston, South Carolina

Library of Congress Control Number: 2011928979

For all general information, please contact Arcadia Publishing:
Telephone 843-853-2070
Fax 843-853-0044
E-mail sales@arcadiapublishing.com
For customer service and orders:
Toll-Free 1-888-313-2665

Visit us on the Internet at www.arcadiapublishing.com

This book is dedicated to the memory of the many pioneers and entrepreneurs whose vision changed a small area of Indiana wilderness into a center of county government, commerce, and industry, inspiring the spirit that keeps the city vibrant today.

CONTENTS

FOREWORD

It has been over 180 years since George King offered to donate 51 acres to the newly formed Johnson County for the purpose of establishing a seat of county government. The commissioners accepted the donation, and Samuel Herriot proposed that the new county seat be named Franklin in honor of Benjamin Franklin. From that virgin plot arose Franklin, beginning as a small-town county seat and gradually evolving into the bustling and thriving "City of Choice" that exists today.

There have been many wonderful moments in Franklin's rich history. In 1824, the first county courthouse was built in downtown Franklin; it was replaced by a larger structure on the town square in 1831. Shortly thereafter, in 1834, the school now known as Franklin College was established on the east side of the city. After fires destroyed earlier courthouses, the current building was erected in 1881, becoming the centerpiece of the downtown landscape. Franklin's first city hall, a beautiful three-story building, was erected in 1895.

The modern city developed in the 20th century. The 1920s saw the construction of the Artcraft Theatre and the dominance of the Wonder Five basketball team. In 1940, *Life* magazine featured Franklin, depicting the perfect example of a small-town Saturday night. Franklin has since grown into a large, third-class city with over 30,000 citizens.

The photographs in this book will take the reader on a tour through the growth of our city. American poet Robert Penn Warren once said, "History cannot give us a program for the future, but it can give us a fuller understanding of ourselves, and of our common humanity, so that we can better face the future."

It is a treat to be a part of this process, to see a book created that highlights the history of our wonderful city. I hope all who read it find a greater appreciation for the city of Franklin. It truly is a wonderful place to live and work. I invite you to visit our city and to experience our piece of Americana.

—Mayor Fred L. Paris
Franklin, Indiana

ACKNOWLEDGMENTS

We could have not even begun this work without the cooperation of the Johnson County Museum of History. The staff and volunteers not only provided us with access to their archives, they became partners in our efforts to search through information and images. We also extend our heartfelt thanks to all who contributed of their time, shared memories, stories, and legends and to those who provided a photograph or two, or just a lead about where to look for information. That list includes many individuals, businesses, religious organizations, the Johnson County Museum of History, City of Franklin employees, Mayor Paris and his staff, Franklin Heritage, Inc., and numerous others.

Among those offering assistance, there are a few that must be thanked individually. Brenna Cundiff, director of the Johnson County Museum of History, assisted us during previous research projects; she and curator Anna Musun-Miller once again opened the museum's archives. In the museum's library, we were joined for untold hours by librarian Linda Talley and her volunteer staff, searching through old texts and seemingly endless files of photographs. The museum staff and volunteers also provided invaluable introductions and contacts with local government offices and business promoters, who each added to the story of the city. Coauthor Jim Hillman was also supported in this work by the University of Phoenix, where he serves as adjunct faculty in the online division. In addition to the above assistance, the people we met all conveyed a remarkable sense of local pride and ownership in their city, an attitude that explains how this community retains the small-town atmosphere that makes it such a desirable home for the citizens.

Unless otherwise noted, all images presented in this book are from the archives of the Johnson County Museum of History.

Of course, none of this would be possible without the support of Kathy and Rita, who allow us the time and encourage us throughout each project and in life every day.

INTRODUCTION

During the 20th century, American painter and illustrator Norman Rockwell depicted small-town and country life on the covers of the *Saturday Evening Post*. Looking at those covers, one could easily envision everyday life in Franklin, Indiana. While it might seem a bit simple—the whole idea of apple pies cooling on the porch or men enjoying a smoke and some gossip in front of the drugstore—Franklin was proudly a small town.

If you ask residents or neighbors from surrounding communities, Franklin encompasses a variety of identities. Historians will discuss the land acquisition from the Delaware Indians, part of the 1818 "New Purchase" agreement. County land went to auction at the land office in Brookville, Indiana, on October 4, 1820. Whetzel Trace, established by Jacob Whetzel and his son Ezra, radiated from Franklin County to the White River Bluffs. Traveling along the Old Indian Trail, the major south-to-north transportation route, settlers arrived in the area, first developing several small communities along the trails and eventually settling along the wooded streams of the central portion of the future Johnson County, where development began as early as 1821.

While many of the early settlers were primarily interested in farmland, others came for more commercial reasons. Indiana had just determined that the city of Indianapolis would become the state capital, a move that would certainly assure business development nearby, so land investors such as George King were drawn to the prospect of rising land values, and men such as John Smiley looked to profit from the need for lumber (which could be produced at Smiley's mill).

Under the leadership of George King, the legislature was moved to establish Johnson County in late 1822, with the new county to be officially established on May 5, 1823. The enabling act of the legislature appointed a board of five commissioners for the new county and directed that they move quickly to establish a seat of government and provide an appropriate public building for the courts.

When the commissioners met in the spring of 1823, there were at least two proposals for the location of the county seat to be considered at existing settlements, but George King came to the meeting and offered to donate just over 50 acres of his land to the county for the county seat. The commissioners accepted his offer, and Samuel Herriot, a prominent resident, proposed that the new town be named Franklin in honor of Benjamin Franklin. The commissioners agreed to the name and hired a surveyor to plat the land into lots, reserving the center for a public square and establishing procedures for the sale of the lots as soon as it was practical.

One can only speculate about the difficulty encountered in attempting to plat lots, streets, and alleys through wooded land with a heavy underbrush, but surveyor David McCaughron, of Bartholomew County, managed to complete the task in a few months. Local legend holds that the bend in Madison Street remains a silent, though perpetual, witness to the intoxicated condition of the surveyor when he laid the lines for that street.

Once the surveyor's work was completed, the commissioners appointed John Campbell as the county agent for sale of the lots. The first sale of lots was advertised for September 2, 1823, and

8

historian David Banta reported, "On that day the county agent, provided with whiskey and paper of the value of $1.18, which the county paid, sold a number of lots adjoining the public square; and on the 14th day of that month exposed to sale other lots." Principal early sales surrounded the public square, with lots selling for amounts ranging from $19 to $40.50.

In 1824, the construction of the first county courthouse, a simple log structure, provided the circuit court with a permanent meeting space and made the town's status as the county seat a practical reality. With growth came the expanding need for more visible law and order, so a brick courthouse was constructed on the public square in 1831. This courthouse was destroyed by fire on May 18, 1849, and was replaced by a third courthouse that was also destroyed by fire (in 1874), resulting in the construction of a temporary courthouse structure that served for seven years. The fifth and current courthouse was readied for occupancy during the summer of 1882.

Academics will point to the arrival of Franklin College as a stabilizing force within the community. Established as a seminary in 1834, the college, founded by pioneering American Baptists, is among Indiana's first liberal arts colleges, as well as the first Indiana college to admit women. By 1850, Franklin's sprawling new Baptist college, diversified industry, productive farming, a county seminary, and a growing faith community—including two Presbyterian congregations, a Baptist church, and a Methodist parish—validated the importance of the town. Indiana governor Roger Branigin and Robert Wise, the director of the film versions of *The Sound of Music* and *West Side Story*, are among Franklin College's distinguished alumni.

With over 250 private housing structures, Franklin grew as the county grew. In the 1850s, a major trail was being built to meet the banks of White River, eventually to extend to Mooresville. With the growing importance of Indianapolis and its location along the transportation route connecting major cities to the south, Franklin was assured to experience continued growth, an expansion evident to this day.

Medical professionals will discuss the impact of Johnson County Memorial Hospital, founded in 1947 as a tribute to the Johnson County men and women who served in World War II. Franklin is also home to two large and historic communities that serve the aging population: the Indiana Masonic Home and the Franklin United Methodist Community. The conversation might also mention Franklin College alumnus George B. Walden, known for his life-saving invention of factory-manufactured insulin.

Leaders in agriculture are quick to focus on the county's family-owned farms, many of which have histories dating into the 1800s. From agriculture to business and industry, Franklin's early economy was powered by the processing of agricultural products and the production of lumber. The 1910s saw the manufacturing of the Continental automobile, followed in the 1920s by other machining operations, and, in the 1930s, the arrival of Noblitt Sparks Industries (later called Arvin Industries). Today, the city's business environment cultivates a diverse mix of agriculture, manufacturing, service, and retailing industries.

The historic preservationists will identify the revitalization of the Artcraft Theatre as the catalyst of Franklin's downtown revitalization. Built in 1922, the theater was originally a silent-movie and vaudeville house. The dressing rooms and stage still exist, as does a recently renovated orchestra pit; in true Franklin tradition, a group of 40 Franklin College students volunteered to excavate 55 cubic yards of sand and concrete that had been used to fill the pit when the theater transitioned to the movie era. In addition, Franklin Heritage, Inc., the local restoration group that currently owns the Artcraft Theatre, continues to restore properties throughout Franklin that have fallen into disrepair. This active local organization uses both professional and volunteer labor to restore and renovate the community. Aside from the courthouse, the city is home to numerous century-old and older homes and buildings. The old Willard Hotel is an active community-gathering place that is beautiful inside and remarkably functional; the upstairs and basement of the hotel serve as a haunted house around Halloween. Built in 1924, the historic Masonic temple building is now home to the Johnson County Museum of History and Johnson County Historical Society, and in the parking lot stands a small, relocated log cabin constructed in 1835 by John and Sally Hendricks. In the city's preserved train station, the Franklin Chamber of Commerce shares quarters with a railroad museum, acknowledging Franklin's importance as a transportation commerce hub. The city offices can be found in the old community opera house.

When talking to residents of Franklin, the word "community" is quick to surface. Through times of economic and natural disasters from fires to floods, the city comes together and rebuilds. Numerous photographs in the archives of the Johnson County Museum of History, as well as pictures and articles represented in the files of area newspapers, show various charity efforts.

A pictorial featuring Franklin, entitled "A Small Town's Saturday Night," appeared in the December 2, 1940, issue of *Life* magazine. According to the magazine's editors, Franklin was the epitome of small-town American life. From rural living to life on the town, readers were invited to experience Franklin. Photographs of cars parked three deep on Jefferson Street and hundreds of people milling about the sidewalks confirm the city's vibrancy.

In his 1941 State of the Union address to the US Congress, Pres. Franklin D. Roosevelt offered the nation his vision for America with four human freedoms: freedom to worship, freedom from fear, freedom from want, and freedom of speech. With simple complexity, Norman Rockwell produced a series of four paintings to soothe a nation in the grips of World War II. Speaking of the freedoms, Roosevelt said, "It is a definite basis for a kind of world attainable in our own time and generation." When examining Rockwell's Four Freedoms, any of the four images could easily be snapshots of Franklin life, for Franklin is not defined by historians, preservationists, academics, businessmen, nor medical professionals, but by her residents.

Franklin today is a Saturday matinee at the Artcraft Theatre, complete with a national anthem reel and classic cartoon, enjoying live music at first Friday on the courthouse square, a late-night drink at a club or coffee shop, and a downtown fall festival parade. The city blossoms during the Johnson County Agricultural Fair in July and becomes aglow in Christmas warmth as the December lights and ornate decorations rise along the downtown streets. Franklin is breakfast at Don and Dona's Restaurant, a stroll along the wooded walks connecting the parks, a swim in the city pool, and an evening seeing a play at Franklin College. But above all else, Franklin is "community."

It is the intent of the authors to accompany the reader on a pictorial journey through time, capturing the unique character of Franklin and its residents. It is not the authors' intent to provide an in-depth, up-to-date, and definitive history of Franklin, an ambitious project yet to be tackled. Through months of research, the authors uncovered many conflicting dates, spelling of names, exact locations of buildings often found to be unknown or disputed, and interviewed people who shared memories that could not be verified. While the authors do not wish to perpetuate inaccuracies, textual decisions sometimes needed to be made in line with the best, most consistent information available. In cases where facts may be in conflict or vivid memories contradicted, please allow the images to tell the story.

One

BEGINNINGS

Although many individuals and events contributed to the formation of Franklin, George King is generally credited as Franklin's founder. King was born in Wythe County, Virginia, eventually settling in Mercer County, Kentucky. He married Eleanor Voorhies and fathered seven children.

In the fall of 1822, King, along with Garrett Bergen and Simon Covert, traveled north to seek land for development in the New Purchase area in central Indiana. After inquiring about a site that might be suitable for a town, King and his partners located the tract lying between Young's Creek and Camp Creek. King acquired 160 acres, and Bergen and Covert each bought 80 acres adjacent to King's property. The land was described as wooded with beech, sugar tree, and poplar timber, as well as a heavy undergrowth of tangled spice brush.

King then took the lead in efforts to get the state legislature to partition a new county, leading to the creation of Johnson County in May 1823. That same month, a commission met at the home of John Smiley to determine a permanent site for the seat of county government; accepting King's proposal to donate 51 acres for the purpose, the commissioners chose to name the new town Franklin and appointed an agent and surveyor to plat the town and begin the sale of lots. The first lots were sold in September 1823.

King was joined by his family and temporarily settled upon a high, dry knoll—a property later donated by King for the establishment of Franklin College. Later, the family constructed a two-room cabin at the present-day intersection of West Jefferson and Walnut Streets. In 1828, King built a modest house on the southwest corner of Main and King Streets and lived at that location until his death on June 26, 1868.

King spent 14 years as postmaster, a term as justice of the peace, was a founding member of the Presbyterian church, served on the board of directors of Franklin College, and was the first president of the Pioneer Cemetery (now the location of Province Park).

FIRST CABIN IN FRANKLIN

A two room log cabin was built on or near this site in March, 1823 by George King, by whose efforts Johnson County was authorized Dec. 31, 1822 and organized March 8, 1823. King donated land for the county seat and Franklin was founded May 22, 1823. King, who came from Kentucky, started the First Presbyterian Church in 1824, served on the first Board of Directors of Franklin College, was a businessman, farmer, postmaster, and Justice of the Peace, died in 1868 and is buried in Greenlawn Cemetery.

ERECTED IN 1973 BY
THE SESQUICENTENNIAL COMMITTEE OF THE JOHNSON COUNTY HISTORICAL SOCIETY

This historical marker, erected at the corner of Jefferson and Walnut Streets, marks the approximate location of George King's first residence. Built at virtually the same time that King donated land for the establishment of the county seat, King's small cabin was the first residence in the new town of Franklin. The King family lived here until they built a new home at Main and King Streets in 1828.

The King family's cabin was not adequate for the size of the family. A new home, constructed in 1828, was more befitting of the King family's continuing prominence in community. As seen in this late-1800s photograph, King's land development efforts paid handsomely and served the family well. Upon his passing in 1868, family heirs made renovations, so the structure seen here is somewhat different from the original construction.

This cabin, constructed in 1835 by Lewis and Sally Hendricks, is the oldest log building still standing in Franklin. Rescued from demolition in the course of development, the cabin now stands in the parking lot of the Johnson County Museum of History. The two-room structure, typical of early cabins, provides visitors with a look at living conditions in the first years of the city.

JOHNSON COUNTY
COURT HOUSES

1st - Court held Smiley's Mill, 5 miles S.E. of Franklin Oct. 16, 1823
2nd - George King home, Franklin, Indiana, March, 1824
3rd - North Main Street, Lot 35, Log, 2 stories, Oct., 1824
4th - Brick, 2 stories, May 5, 1832. Burned - May 18, 1849
5th - Brick, 2 stories, 1849. Burned Dec. 12, 1874
6th - Frame, located S.E. corner Monroe and Main Streets 1875-1881

Present Court House built 1879 to 1881, accepted by County Commissioners Dec. 1881. Cost $100,000.00.

MARKER ERECTED 1964 — JOHNSON COUNTY HISTORICAL SOCIETY

The historical marker standing on the courthouse lawn recounts the history of the various buildings that housed the courts. While George King's dreams for Johnson County had been greatly realized during his lifetime, the visible history of the county's legal seat continued after his passing. Located on land now occupied by the Artcraft Theatre, the 1824 log courthouse was the first public structure in Johnson County.

During Franklin's centennial celebration, a parade float carries a model of the first courthouse; the banner states that the building also housed the first public school in 1829. While plausible, as the courthouse was the only public building in the community, it may have been utilized for education, but few records substantiate that the courthouse space was used as a schoolhouse.

Organized religion continues to be an important component of Franklin life. A Presbyterian congregation was founded by George King and a handful of others in 1824. Most of the families migrated from Mercer County, Kentucky. It is interesting to note that at this same time, another group of migrants from Mercer County, Kentucky, founded a Presbyterian congregation in the town of Greenwood in the northern part of Johnson County.

The charter members of First Presbyterian were George King and family, Joseph and Nancy Gilcress, and King's son-in-law David McCaslin. The Presbyterian congregation flourished and outgrew its meetinghouse within 20 years. The members replaced the inadequate facility with a large and imposing church (above). As membership continued to grow, the church building was demolished and, using the original bricks, a larger replacement facility (right) was fully operational by 1878. This facility, located on the corner of Water and Madison Streets, is a far cry from the King cabin where the plans for a Presbyterian community were first discussed.

Aside from the prolific Presbyterian congregation, Franklin attracted several faith communities. Bethel African Methodist Episcopal Church was founded in Philadelphia in 1787 and established in Franklin in 1868. The modest white structure pictured above was the Bethel AME church, completed in 1911 to serve the primarily African American congregation. Methodists, Anglican Catholics, Roman Catholics, and various other Christian denominations were well represented. In 1838, town founder George King sold a parcel of land at the southeast corner of Jefferson Street and Home Avenue to the First Baptist Church. Later, the Second Baptist Church and the Franklin First Separate Baptist Church, seen below, arrived to serve the community.

WILLIAM WATSON WICK
1796-1868

born in Cannonsburg, PA, came to Indiana in 1819; elected Clerk of the Indiana House of Representatives in 1820; chosen first Judge of the New Purchase in 1822; first Judge to hold court in Indianapolis; held first court in Johnson County at John Smiley's cabin, Oct. 16, 1823; Johnson County Circuit Judge, intermittently until 1859; elected Indiana Secretary of State (1825-1829); served three terms in the U. S. Congress; was an 1849 Presidential Elector; Indianapolis Postmaster, 1853-1857; nearly forty years in public life.

While George King gets much of the notice for the founding of Franklin, this historic marker recalls another prominent figure, Judge William Watson Wick. Wick was the presiding judge of the judicial circuit during the time the county was founded, and he played a significant planning and organizational role within county government and during construction of the courthouse. Wick was the first judge to hold court in Johnson County. (Authors' collection.)

Col. Sam P. Oyler was born in England in 1819 and arrived in Franklin in 1834. Oyler served under General Sherman during the Civil War. He returned to Franklin after the war to practice law with his stepson Daniel. The Oyler family was well known in Franklin. Oyler served as Franklin's mayor from 1892 to 1894.

John Terrell Vawter was a noted Franklin businessman. His dealings in real estate, including Vawter Park Village and Vawter Park Hotel, which made up the first development on the south shore of Indiana's Lake Wawasee, made Vawter a wealthy man. His Franklin interests included a well-known meatpacking operation. Vawter financed and donated the Vawter Civil War Memorial on Franklin's courthouse square.

Transportation of people and merchandise, whether in town, on the farm, or traveling between towns, depended on horsepower. Franklin had a few livery stables that provided a place for a town dweller to stable his animals and often a place where a visitor might be able to rent a horse or carriage while staying in town. This c. 1883 picture depicts the Wolfe and Valentine Livery, Feed, and Sale Stable.

The photograph above shows the sprawling B. Jacob's Livery Stable in 1880. The stables were high-demand, year-round operations. As one of the largest transportation businesses in Franklin, B. Jacob directly competed with Wolfe and Valentine for Franklin-area customers. There were also a dozen or so smaller stable businesses. Jarve Alexander Livery Stable, seen in the 1885 photograph below, was one of the smaller competitors. Alexander's business survived the transition from horse and buggy to horseless carriage, operating several transportation-related businesses in Franklin. Aside from providing stables, feed, and general repair services, many livery stables also employed veterinarians, blacksmiths, and carriages for hire.

In this mid-1800s image taken from a southeast viewpoint—one of the earliest known photographs of Franklin—wagons negotiate a messy West Jefferson Street after a rainstorm. The settlement of Franklin had occurred nearly a quarter of a century earlier, and within that short time the downtown area had rapidly developed with multiple homes and business buildings, yet the roadway and walkways were still very primitive. The streets were well defined, even having stone curbs in many locations with the rock and hard surface pavement, but adequate drainage was not a common feature. The drivers often stood in the carriages to watch for road hazards and to gain better control of the horses. While downtown streets posed numerous obstacles, the routes into town were even more treacherous. The streets would need dramatic improvements in the following years, especially with the advent of motor vehicles in the 1900s.

Pictured above is Stott Hall, commonly known as Old Main. In 1834, with the town barely a decade old, a group of American Baptists founded a small seminary on the east side of Franklin called the Franklin Manual Labor Institute. Originally, the college consisted of one log cabin but began adding larger facilities, most notably Chandler Hall in 1844 and Baily Hall in 1854; both preceded the construction of the Old Main landmark structure, which was ready for use in 1895. In 1842, the school began to admit women, becoming the first coeducational institution in Indiana and the seventh in the nation. Even with the population of female students walking the halls, Franklin College closed during the Civil War and reopened in 1869. The postcard view below shows the early Franklin College library building.

Nearly from the beginning, the Johnson County Fair has been an anticipated event for area residents. Johnson County's first fair was held in November 1838 in Garrett C. Bergen's woods, the area now known as Martin Place. Entrance to the temporary fairgrounds bumped against North Main Street at the location noted by the historical marker shown above. In 1867, the fair found a home that remains the current and permanent site of the fairgrounds. Below, at the new fairgrounds, a group of horsemen take a moment between races to pose for the camera. The annual celebration of agriculture charged no admission fee and was always well attended. (Above, authors' collection.)

Entertainment at local fairs and parades was often provided by groups such as the military band pictured above. There was little available in the way of in-home entertainment, so it was common for families to spend evenings in the town square socializing with their neighbors, while local bands played for the public on weekends. Along with local school performance groups, including Franklin College talent, the 4-H band, and various big band and contemporary performers, the military band was among the big draws. Below is a community memorial to James C. Mansfield, leader of the Franklin Military Band, as seen on December 29, 1884.

For a more formal evening of entertainment, groups like this glee club would perform at the local opera house or appear at events sponsored by church groups and similar organizations. The dress of this club, shown here in 1875, illustrates that they are cultured and formal—not likely to appear at an open-air fair or festival gathering.

Instrumental groups such as the mandolin club in this 1880 photograph were often sponsored by church or civic organizations primarily to provide a form of entertainment for their members. These groups provided their members with a wholesome way to socialize with others who had similar interests, a genteel alternative to gathering at a local tavern or playing a card game.

Franklin's county-seat status was a natural attraction for business, so the downtown area, especially the streets surrounding the public square, began to sprout rows of commercial buildings. The part of Jefferson Street seen here illustrates the typical construction, featuring a retail space on the street level with room for offices on the upper floors. Shopping and business all took place downtown in the 1800s.

On the outskirts and throughout the town, there was a growth in middle-class housing, as seen in this photograph of the home of Wilson T. Hougham Sr., in Needham Township. Pictured in 1875, Hougham (center front) poses with his wife, Mary, and sons, Charles and Edward, in front of the house. In the background is Nora Franklin, who also made her home with the family.

This 1878 bird's-eye view of the town of Franklin provides a dramatic illustration of the growth of the town. Founded only 55 years earlier on 51 acres of native wooded land, it was now covered by buildings large and small, including public buildings, churches, businesses, and homes. The two waterways that once were deer runs were now pleasant greenways through the town, easily crossed by bridges at the main roads—Franklin was truly coming of age. While the early days of Franklin's development were haphazard at best, the town fathers eventually platted the central area into 90 lots after some difficulty locating original buildings due to flooding. The center of town was divided by Main Street, and four blocks were reserved as the public square, eventually the location of the current courthouse. Lost within the illustration is George King's original cabin just west of the public square at Jefferson and Walnut Streets.

John Smiley migrated to New Purchase land in 1822 and, like King, came not for farming but for commercial interests. Smiley erected the first lumber mill in the area, shown in this early photograph. Smiley was appointed the first sheriff of the new county, and the first court session was held in his home in 1823.

Early commercial development in Franklin was focused on services to the surrounding farms. As the land around the town was gradually cleared and converted for farming, grain elevators and feed mills such as the one pictured above began to appear as early as 1825 and remained viable businesses for over a century.

Suckow Mill and Elevator, Franklin, Ind.

The Suckow and Company Mill was one of the most prominent business structures in Franklin. William Suckow arrived in Franklin from the mills in Wisconsin and purchased an interest in the McDaniel and Company Mill in 1888. Eventually, the entire business became his operation, and he was shipping nearly 10,000 barrels per day of his Perfection Flour brand made from wheat purchased from local farmers. The postcard view above shows Suckow Mill shortly after opening, while the more recent photograph below is notated as "Union Roller Mill, William Suckow, proprietor." Serving primarily East Coast and Southern consumers, the mill also processed corn and other bran products, and it even included some dairy operations. By 1952, economics had changed, and the Suckow Mill was replaced by a shopping center.

Single-family homes were built near the Suckow Mill (far right) and became a source of potential mill employees. According to an advertising poem of unknown origin, "A worthy home industry, deserving of your trade, is the Union Roller Mills, for the fame their flour has made. Wm. Suckow is well known, and understands the trade, and manufactures several brands, of flour of finest grade."

Since agriculture was Franklin's primary trade, along with the mills, grain elevators, and feed operations, the canning businesses prospered into the 1900s. In this rare 1890s photograph, hardworking women label cans packed with local harvests. Note that while the women work, the men—apparently the supervisors—stand.

As the 1800s came to an end, it seemed as if the two governments, city and county, were competing to see which could complete the most visible construction project. In the center of the public square stands the new courthouse (above), built in 1881–1882 at a cost of over $100,000. This building, which still stands today, is the last of five courthouses that the county built in a period of less than 75 years. The first courthouse was replaced to gain space, two later buildings were destroyed by fire, and one was intended to serve as a temporary structure until the existing building was erected. A few years after the new county courthouse was completed, the city embarked on the construction of the first city hall (below). The impressive three-story stone and brick structure was completed and occupied by city offices in 1895. The building, located directly across the street from the county courthouse, effectively brought all area government offices to the public square.

Two

GROWTH BRINGS PROSPERITY

Throughout the 1800s, Franklin transformed from a town into a city. With the impressive new courthouse and city offices anchoring the community, continued growth was secure. The interurban, serving as a complement to train service, fueled economics and connected Franklin to both Indianapolis and Louisville. Along with trains and the interurban, the J.H. Bus Line provided another way for Franklin residents and businesses to stay connected with emerging developments.

Personal transportation evolved from horse to horseless carriages. Resident Gilbert VanVleet drove his 1901 Oldsmobile through downtown, a first for the city; streetscapes changed rapidly, with cars replacing horses at a gallop. By 1909, Franklin's Indiana Motor Manufacturing Company was ready to produce its line of Continental vehicles.

To meet personal transportation needs, the hub of downtown Franklin saw the refinement of downtown offerings, including gas and vehicle service centers, traveler services, retail, and restaurants. Local industry was flourishing, evident with activity at the local mills and production facilities, including agricultural processing and canning, lumber distribution, and even desk production. Jobs were mostly plentiful and income was on the rise, marked by rapid expansion of housing options.

In 1906, the *Daily Star* became the *Evening Star* and served the newspaper needs of the community, facing little competition until the *Daily Journal* arrived in 1963. Enterprising businessmen, along with the city, developed, maintained, and managed the gas, electric, water, and telephone infrastructure of Franklin, frequently making investments in new service delivery methods. The city installed a modern sewage system in 1905.

Franklin College was developing a national reputation for academics. The Masons and other fraternal and civic organizations enhanced the community, offering various opportunities to serve others. The opera house, and later the Artcraft Theatre, along with the development of parkland, provided just a few of the many leisure options for Franklin residents. Many festivals, fairs, and celebrations brought a sense of unity and identity to the area. Enhancements to public education, the continued attraction and development of faith communities, and the provision of quality public services solidified the city's desirability. Franklin was definitely coming of age within the central Indiana region.

The interurban, an efficient electric-powered rail system, began operation in 1900. The Franklin interurban station was conveniently located downtown at the corner of Madison and Main Streets. The interurban is pictured making a Franklin stop in the postcard view above. Below, the interurban rails are shown in the winter; the interurban was able to safely transport passengers during periods of snow or rain. The *Dixie Flyer*, traveling from Indianapolis to Louisville, was a popular route along the line. Between Indianapolis and Louisville, Columbus and Franklin were among the most popular stops. The primary utility of the interurban route was conveniently transporting Franklin residents to and from Indianapolis's Traction Terminal for work. The interurban ceased operations in 1945.

In this image from 1930, a crowd of excited ticket holders watches as the *Southwind* streaks into the old Pennsylvania Rail Road depot for the very first time. By this time, transportation by horse and carriage was a rare sight; with the proliferation of trains, the interurban, buses, taxis, and personal vehicles, the battle for horsepower had been won by the machines. Franklin was home to three train stations serving the interurban, the Madison-Indianapolis Line, and the Big Four. The Big Four Depot was located at the east end of Martin Place, serving the Cincinnati and Mahalasville line, crossing Main and Adams Streets and exiting town at Walnut and West Jefferson Streets. All that remains of Franklin's rich railroad legacy can be found in the rail beds throughout town and the restored, but relocated, Big Four depot, now the Franklin Chamber of Commerce office and railroad museum.

Old Main symbolizes the very essence of Franklin College. The tower is stately and upholds the promise of a liberal arts education. Literature, art, philosophy, and all the world's disciplines offer a new and exciting life outside the safety of the Franklin community. When the original Old Main burned on April 21, 1985, there was no doubt the structure would be rebuilt.

Franklin could be considered the knowledge capital of Johnson County. The Franklin College Library is depicted on this old postcard. Along with the college library, Franklin has a local public library constructed through the aid of a Carnegie grant. For the population of Franklin, well-stocked libraries are true community assets. The Johnson County Library system originated in Franklin and now serves several Johnson County communities.

While most buildings on the Franklin College campus were grand Colonial brick structures, this 1918 photograph depicts the college mess hall. The building served many purposes during its existence, even housing soldiers at one time. The building became an even greater eyesore with age and acquired a reputation of being haunted.

A relaxing time with old friends and food defines this late-1800s Franklin Township School District No. 1 reunion. Classmates would travel from near and far to experience the nostalgia of the reunions. Today, attendance at class reunions is not seen as a priority, but at the dawn of the 20th century, a class reunion was the only way for people to reestablish contact with old friends.

The 1939 Delta Delta Delta pledges pose together for a group photograph. Pledges were solicited by current members and usually withstood a grueling battery of tests and a final initiation. Only a limited number of girls were allowed to pledge, and competition could be fierce. Fraternity and sorority life had many demands but also many benefits, including a strong network of brothers and sisters.

This winter photograph depicts the Sigma Alpha Epsilon house, located at 800 East Jefferson Street near the Franklin College campus. Fraternity and sorority life is and has long been an important component of college. Many fraternity and sorority houses, large and elaborate structures, coexist amid the homes and neighborhood businesses in Franklin.

The Holstein Grocery (above) was located on East Jefferson Street, neighboring the old Rairdon Building. Operated by Altis and Daisy Fry, the store opened in 1913. McGinnis Grocery (below) was also located on East Jefferson Street. While the East Jefferson Street location was home base, the McGinnis family owned and operated three locations. Competitors included Alford's Grocery Store at 701 Johnson Avenue, Sam Swiggett's store at Cincinnati and Duane Streets, Demaree's on East Jefferson Street, and a host of others. The grocery stores were small, customer-driven operations, and product lines varied by neighborhood. Some stores offered home deliveries or credit by handshake. As the larger chain grocery stores came to town, the small grocers slowly disappeared.

JOHNSON COUNTY HISTORICAL MUSEUM   FRANKLIN, INDIANA
150 West Madison Street   Home Given by Suckow Family

The Johnson County Museum of History had humble beginnings as service work by the Daughters of the American Revolution (DAR). The county museum had quarters in the basement of the courthouse until 1963, when Clara Suckow donated a house and property at 150 West Madison Street (above). Rachel Henry became curator in 1972, making a formal collaboration with the county's historical society a possibility; in 1980, the Johnson County Historical Society assumed operational control. In 1988, the Johnson County Historical Society acquired Franklin Masonic Temple, a suitable home for the organization's growing collection, for $120,000 and raised $600,000 in additional funds for renovations. Ground-breaking for the Masonic temple took place on March 22, 1922 (below). The building is listed on the National Register of Historic Places.

The Masonic Temple building (right) was dedicated on April 14, 1924. The structure, noted for its Ionic columns and Neoclassical stylings, was designed by Evansville's Clifford Shopbell, from the architectural firm of Shopbell, Fowler, and Thole, and cost $104,000. After the county and historical society acquired the property, the Hendricks's cabin was restored and relocated to the museum's grounds from Needham Township. The museum holds many special events. The auditorium (below) is ideal for larger gatherings. Permanent exhibits include Native American and European Travelers, Pioneer Settlers, Indiana Infantry in the Civil War, and Victorian Life. Special exhibits are also planned throughout the year.

The Masonic Temple is not only a historic building, it has played host to numerous historic occasions. The organizational meeting of the Franklin Kiwanis Club took place at the temple, an event depicted in this 1925 image. The Masonic building hosted a variety of community events and was a preferred meeting place in town.

While the Masonic Temple held landmark status in town, this iconic entry gate and dual arches welcomed people to the Indiana Masonic Home. Neighboring Franklin College on the city's south side, the Indiana Masonic Home cornerstone was laid on October 21, 1915. An inclusive community quickly arose from the woods and fields to serve orphaned children, the elderly, and the needy.

Boys' Cottage, Indiana Masonic Home, Franklin, Ind.

The Masonic Home included the Indiana Masons Widows and Orphans Home, complete with a school, training programs, and residential facilities. The boys' cottage (above), one of the girls' cottages (below), and additional residential facilities housed hundreds of children over the years. Once the children were grown and ready to venture beyond the stone arches, the alumni were well prepared to begin life with completed educational coursework and vocational training. The complex has maintained a large and well-equipped hospital, a health-care center, furnished apartments, cottages, and multiple dining facilities. While the school has closed and most of the orphans are gone, the elder care facilities remain ready to serve Indiana's aging Masonic population.

Girls' Cottage No. 2, Indiana Masonic Home, Franklin, Ind.

The size of the sprawling Indiana Masonic Home complex is depicted in this modern aerial view. The facility has been a strong economic catalyst since inception, employing numerous medical personnel, teachers, social workers, and support personnel. On October 28, 1916, the Indiana Masonic Home was dedicated and began accepting residents. Since its inception, the Indiana Masonic Home has provided living services for nearly 10,000 adults and over 800 children. Known as the "Home Kids," many live at the facility today. All in all, the Indiana Masonic Home provides residential services for 400 family members. Recently, the home added a memory care program. According to official literature, "Freemasonry always has inculcated lessons of love and helpfulness that reach out toward the unfavored and unfortunate, especially to the aged Mason, the widow and the orphan. Around its Altars are taught the tenets of Brotherly Love, Relief and Truth that find expression in pure benevolence of which the Indiana Masonic Home is a noble example."

42

The US Postal Service proudly served the residents of Franklin. A well-dressed and very photogenic team of postal employees poses above outside the Franklin Post Office in 1906. Below, postal trucks line up in front of the Franklin Main Street office; the Artcraft Theatre is visible on the left side of the photograph. At that time, Franklin employed five letter carriers: H. Craig, C. Barnum, Wayne Walters, J. Patterson, and Bill Clark, who are seen standing by their delivery trucks. George King's cabin served as the area's first post office. Postal services were located in several downtown storefronts until a post office was constructed at West Madison and Jackson Streets. The post office remained at that location until moving to a new facility on North Main Street in 1980.

The need for a community library was recognized by 1900; however, funds were not raised until 1911. On the second floor of a downtown building, located on the southwest corner of Jefferson and Walnut Streets, Franklin's new public library opened above Betty's Restaurant but was soon lost to fire. A new public library, funded with $17,500 from a Carnegie grant, opened in 1916 at the corner of Madison Street and Home Avenue. The Franklin Public Library (at left and below) became the Franklin-Johnson County Library in the late 1970s and now is referred to as Johnson County Public Library. The system currently has four branches and a service center. The Franklin branch, located near the historic Indiana Masonic Home entrance, opened on State Street in late 1988; Johnson County Public Library is seeking to move and then expand the Franklin branch to the outskirts of town.

Public Library, Franklin, Ind.

Religion was an important aspect of Franklin life. The Tabernacle Christian Church was originally established as the Franklin Christian Church. Built at the conclusion of the 18th century at King and Water Streets, the church moved and expanded several times. The current church is pictured above, and the structure, unique in architecture, is guaranteed to be spotted when traveling through Franklin's downtown neighborhood. The Queen Esther Sunday school class of Tabernacle Christian Church is pictured below after services in 1929. Specialized groups within congregations were popular in area churches. Bible study groups, choirs, missions, and community outreach programs flourished.

The Booker T. Washington School (above) served Franklin's African American student population. Operating under the assumption that the school was "separate but equal" to the "white" schools, students were taught by well-educated African American teachers. In 1900, over 20 children of varying ages attended the school, often sharing the same classrooms and lessons. Teacher Nettie Craft (below, standing at left) watches over her botany class during the 1904–1905 school year at Franklin High School. The first schools in Franklin were conducted in private homes, and some churches provided private school, but public education was not formalized until a school was built in the early 1930s. For those seeking a professional occupation, a trade academy prospered on West Jefferson Street for several years.

Franklin High School, Franklin, Indiana.

The new Alva Neal High School, also known as Franklin High School—the crown jewel of the Franklin school system—opened in 1910 and served the school system until the late 1970s. Located on Hurricane Street at the east end of Madison Street, the building has served many functions since ending use as a school. Currently, the structure is known as the Alva Neal Community Office Building and is home to several small independent businesses and public spaces.

The Franklin College bicycle team poses for a photograph in the early 1900s. Franklin students were known for riding bikes to class and through town. The Grizzly Grand Prix, an annual bicycle race sponsored by Franklin College, has been held on the track of Goodell Field, as well as on the Indiana Masonic Home's circular drive.

This photograph from 1900 features Franklin College students playing a friendly game of football. Considering the small size of the college, an organized and competitive football team was an extracurricular rarity. Today, games are played at Goodell Field, home of the Grizzlies.

Pictured with a football in 1901 are, from left to right, Mark Webb, Verne Branigan, and Mark Miller, who were among Franklin College's talented players. While football was the most popular Grizzly sport, basketball games also drew enthusiastic crowds. Given the success of Franklin High School's basketball program, the whole town of Franklin had sports fever!

Basketball was popular in Franklin. The 1922–1923 Franklin High School team is shown in this photograph. The team followed a tradition of competitive play, including the victorious "Wonder Five" and their 1920, 1921, and 1922 Indiana state championships. The Cubs brought great pride to Franklin. The 1922–1923 team faced high expectations for the season, but a state championship that year was not in the cards.

Franklin College also had an active tennis team called the Hercules Tennis Club; players were very competitive on the courts. The college was committed to offering extracurricular tennis and invested in building the courts and maintaining them for student and faculty use. While popular at Franklin College in the 1920s, tennis was just beginning to take root as a player and spectator sport across the country.

All pomp and circumstance greeted the 1909 graduating class of Franklin College. During the early 1900s, the college graduated about 30 students annually. Men far outnumbered women when it came to receiving diplomas from the institution. The college served mostly middle-class white males.

High school graduating classes were small. Many students did not finish their high school educations, opting instead to work in business or in the fields. Several students forfeited the high school experience in order to support their families. Only three males graduated in this early-1900s class, which also contained two African American graduates.

Even in the early 1900s, Franklin had an active chamber of commerce. The Franklin Chamber of Commerce Board of Directors is depicted in this 1920s portrait. Several important community leaders were associated with the chamber, including recognizable surnames like Alexander, Suckow, Hougham, Graham, Owens, and Payne. In 1923, the organization had 240 individual members and 44 corporate partners listed on its rolls.

For Franklin residents, end-of-life matters were frequently handled by A.V. Vandivier and Sons Funeral Services. In this 1925 image, A.V. Vandivier (left) and Riehl Vandivier prepare to make a house call. More than likely, the Vandiviers would prepare the deceased for burial at convenient Greenlawn Cemetery.

Even with development happening in Franklin during the early 1900s, the serenity of nature could still be found within walking distance. While the sounds of trains and cars could be heard in the distance, the hustle and bustle of city life could easily be forgotten, if only for a brief time. Above, an old iron railroad bridge overlooks an untamed Young's Creek in winter. Young's Creek had a history of unmanageable flooding, usually in late spring or early fall. The land near the creek was often muddy and thick with uncontained growth and had gnarled trees protruding from the banks in every direction, as shown below. During the quiet of summer, fishing and wading were common, simple pastimes.

The newspaper was an important aspect of small-town life throughout the 1900s. The Johnson County *Examiner* first hit area newsstands in 1845. The first major "must-read" Franklin paper was the *Democrat*. This image presents a rare glimpse of the interior of *Democrat* offices during the early years of the paper. The *Democrat* office was located at 49 South Water Street.

The *Daily Star* first appeared in the mid-1860s. Although several newspapers were published in Franklin over the years, the *Daily Star* was the most successful. Eventually the paper was renamed the *Evening Star* and became the only paper in town. The *Daily Journal* arrived in Franklin in the early 1960s, and within a few years, the *Evening Star* closed down.

The courthouse was the catalyst for the creation of multiple public safety, legal, and support service jobs and businesses. The Huddleston Law Office on West Jefferson Street was one such business. Law offices and legal services were numerous in Franklin, and most operations were concentrated on the streets near the courthouse.

The sheriff served an important and necessary role within every community and was well rewarded for keeping the city streets safe. The Johnson County sheriff's residence stood in the shadow of the busy Knights of Pythias Building, centrally located and highly visible to downtown visitors.

This candid 1924 image memorializes two popular Franklin police officers: John C. Bergen (left) and Lum Harrison. Franklin police offers were required to live within the Franklin community. Most residents knew the police officers by name, as they were the same folks who lived in the neighborhood, attended church services, shopped in downtown stores, and saw movies at the Artcraft Theatre.

Dave Kelley's house was also Dave Kelley's greenhouse operation. The residence and business was a true work-at-home situation. Even in the early 1900s, a house located near the center of town with a greenhouse in the backyard was an odd sight. In modern society, with all the residential zoning laws enacted, Dave Kelley's greenhouse operation would not be permitted.

Fires plagued early Franklin. This photograph shows the spectacular fire that destroyed the Mutual Building and Loan on Water Street in 1936. The firefighters were to be commended for saving the surrounding businesses. With businesses located so close to each other, often in adjoining structures, fires could easily spread and destroy entire city blocks.

Pictures of old banking businesses prove interesting because there have been so many changes in the industry. This image depicts the interior of the Farmer's Trust Bank located at the corner of Water and Jefferson Streets. A Western Union telegraph office shared part of the building. In later years, Farmer's Trust Bank experienced several name changes, including Franklin Bank and Trust, Ameritrust, and Key Bank.

The Franklin Desk Company was a successful manufacturing business with a national reputation for quality and innovation. The desk factory had a relatively large workforce and served Franklin well as a community partner. The management of the company valued the employees and understood the necessary balance between work and family. In the 1920s, the desk factory was destroyed in a major fire; the business was unable to recover. Before the fire, Franklin Desk Company had begun to lose its competitive edge. Being located in Franklin, Indiana, had many challenges, including securing quality raw materials to use in producing quality products.

The smokestacks at Hoagland's Canning Factory were visible for miles around the facility. Manufacturing and industrial plants dotted the rural landscape, locating close to the source of materials or simply where land could be bought at a low price. Later, industrial sites were located in industrial parks, where they could be served by improved roadways, rail service, and similar utilities.

These gentlemen kept the canning machinery in excellent shape. When a production line malfunctioned, both time and money were immediately lost. This rare image portrays the interior of the machine shop. Machine repair was a lucrative career field, and several jobs were available in the factories and industrial plants of Franklin.

Horse-and-buggy travel increasingly became obsolete through the 1920s. Road construction and drainage control became a necessity as Franklin streets transitioned to providing adequate roadways for new modes of mechanized transportation. Unfortunately, newly paved streets with drainage into local waterways accelerated the flooding of local streams during periods of rain.

Franklin resident Maurice Johnson is pictured here near the courthouse in 1922. Making his downtown rounds via horses and carriage, Johnson encountered modern automobiles, taxis, trains, and the interurban. Even by 1922, traditional horsepower was seldom seen in downtown Franklin; however, townspeople could occasionally spot a farmer picking up supplies or hauling a harvest to markets and factories.

The W.H. Younce Shoe Store on West Jefferson Street was one of the most popular footwear stores in the city. The interior of the Younce Shoe Store is seen in the early-1900s image above. Sam Lanam purchased the well-stocked store from Younce, later retiring and leaving the business to Russell Yount, Lanam's son-in-law. Yount's son became the next proprietor when his father passed. During the later years of the business, Lanam's Shoes moved to a strip mall on the outskirts of town, was streamlined, and became Lanam's Buster Brown Shoes, seen below. Considering the number of department stores and independent shoe stores in Franklin, the local market provided considerable competition. Given three generations of ownership, Lanam's successful Franklin run was commendable.

Through the steadfast efforts of the Franklin chapter of the DAR, soldiers buried in Johnson County's Greenlawn Cemetery are not just recognized, but honored. The Daughters embarked on a project to memorialize the fallen, unsung heroes of America's past. This simple but highly visible rock contains an embedded plaque that acknowledges the lost lives of soldiers.

Keeping the grounds tidy was important to the Patterson Store on North Main Street. When the store closed, a barbershop opened in the building. Corner barbershops were bustling places where men gathered for a haircut, a cup of coffee, and fellowship. Franklin had several neighborhood shops in the early 1950s, including Winchester's Barber Shop on Court Street and Goldsmith's Barber Shop on North Main Street.

Located at 20 North Main Street, the Franklin Pharmacy was a central location to catch lunch or a quick Coca-Cola, either at the lunch counter or by car curb service. The advertising slogan, "2't your horn 2wice for curb service," would work well in modern texting society. The pharmacy was popular with the teenage crowd.

Henry Surface's shoe shop was located on the southwest corner of Jefferson Street near the courthouse; the business was known for speedy and quality shoe shines. Sandefurs Lunch Room shared the building with the shoe store and was a popular eating spot amongst the legal and professional crowd. Of interest is a billboard to the left promoting the "Miracle Man."

Next to a Lloyd's Laundry truck, a contrasting horse-and-wagon team is seen delivering shipments of a tasty Franklin original, Double Cola. Ralph Harmon, a grocer by trade, began the Franklin Bottling Company in the back room of his Holstein building on the 400 block of East Jefferson Street.

The soda-bottling operation monopolized most of Harmon's time. The back of his grocery store was no longer sufficient given the growing popularity of his bottled drinks. A new factory was constructed at the corner of Wayne and Water Streets. With the new building and increased production capacity, Franklin Bottling Company was able to triple output.

By the early 1920s, the Franklin Bottling Company had retired most of the horse and delivery wagon fleet, opting for more efficient delivery trucks, shown above stocked for deliveries. Led by the popularity of Harmon's Wonder Orange drink, Jumbo Cola became the company's best seller. Harmon created several drink recipes, including Wonder Orange, Black Cherry, Lemon Sur, and others. Considering sales of all Franklin Bottling Company flavors, Double Cola stole the top spot from Jumbo Cola. With brisk Double Cola sales, Harmon changed the company name to Double Cola Bottling Company. The company closed in the 1980s. Below, a later-model Double Cola truck makes a delivery.

In an old brick building at 354 East Monroe Street, the Alexander brothers developed an ice-manufacturing plant. Previous building occupants included a wool mill and Civil War blanket-making facility, the Coil Hoop Company that manufactured metal security hoops for kegs and barrels, and a lumber mill. The ice plant closed in the late 1950s.

In the early 1900s, Franklin was chosen as the site of a new automobile-production facility. The Continental vehicle was heavily promoted in the area, as seen in this photograph of a display at the Johnson County Fair. The vehicle was only produced for four years. The sign promises the car will start, but will it run?

The Continental was a sharp-looking cruiser. The vehicle was entered into competition at the Indianapolis 500 but did not qualify. The minimum speed at the "Brickyard" was 75 miles per hour, a speed that was difficult for the Continental to achieve. Despite receiving mixed reviews by owners, the cars were relatively reliable.

Red Cross workers pose for a photograph at the Johnson County Fairgrounds during World War I. The year 1918 was a busy time in the city. Franklin College and the fairgrounds both served roles during the conflicts. Facilities at both locations were used for housing needs and supply storage. The city of Franklin played a major support role during both world wars.

Outdoor recreational opportunities were plentiful in Franklin. Golfing, horseback riding, bicycling, outdoor organized sports, and other warm-weather activities were available to Franklin residents. Swimming was popular in the city. The private swimming pool at the Franklin Country Club (above) served the city's most affluent and elite. While men were playing golf, women and children would hit the pool. Franklin also had a large municipal pool (below). Although it is pictured here in the off-season, the city pool was often packed during the summer months. At times, the pool had to limit admissions due to crowding and safety concerns. When the old pool closed, a new aquatic center was built in the main city park, convenient to the Indiana Masonic Home, Franklin College, and the downtown area.

FRANKLIN MEMORIAL SWIMMING POOL, FRANKLIN, IND.   E-565

Franklin residents always enjoy a good celebration. From parades to street fairs and live music on the courthouse square, downtown played host to a variety of events. In a review of history, Franklin's centennial celebration was by far the most popular and well-documented city gathering. Above, downtown streets are being readied for a celebration. Below, after the work is complete, a midway spectacular draws a crowd with a colorful electric Eli Wheel. Franklin was no stranger to traveling carnivals, as the fair regularly provided such offerings, including the most spectacular and newest portable rides. The lights, sounds, and smell of the midway drew crowds from miles around Franklin. In recent years, the Johnson County Fair has used the family-owned Poor Jack Amusements to provide rides and games during the annual event. This show is noted for continually adding new attractions while maintaining affordable ticket prices and a sterling safety record.

Franklin residents did not need grand, elaborate events to join with neighbors for socializing. This 1902 photograph shows ladies coming together for a card party. These parties were usually held in the afternoons and consisted of a little friendly competition along with light refreshments and some obligatory gossip.

Fun and business do mix. At the Johnson County Fair, businesses often assembled exciting displays to spotlight new services and products. Under this commercial tent, visitors find the latest advances in farming implements. While commercial offerings attracted the attention of fairgoers, exhibit space was leased to provide the fair board with another much-needed revenue stream.

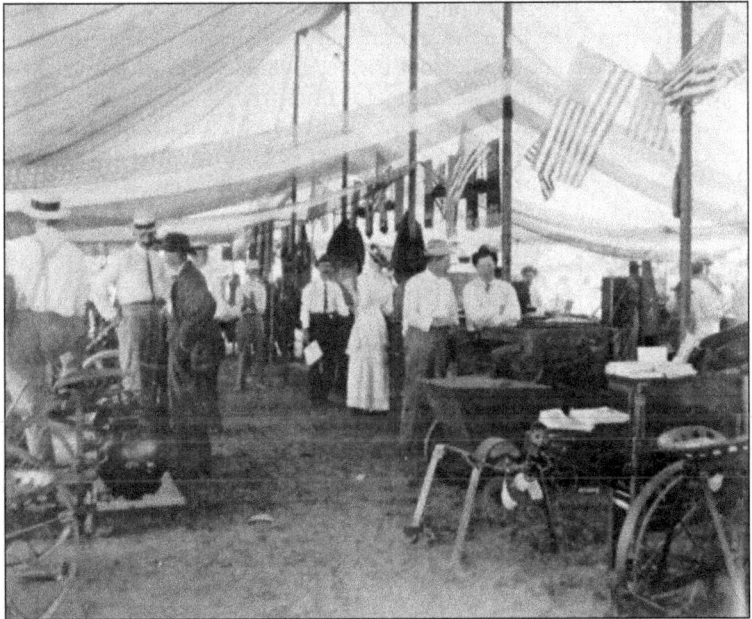

An Easter egg hunt in the park in the 1950s continues the small-town tradition of family-friendly, community-based recreational activities. Beginning as a mostly rural community, a trip to town or a gathering at the church were times for socializing and meeting with friends and neighbors, providing a welcome break from the relative isolation of farm life. As the town grew into a city, and the population became more concentrated into neighborhoods rather than farms, the city parks became public gathering places used by many organizations as spaces for open-air recreational events. The parks provided grassy fields for events like this one, as well as baseball diamonds, tennis courts, and other amenities for public use. Seasonal activities were sponsored by churches and civic organizations

The city spared no effort in 1923 to celebrate the 100th anniversary of Franklin's founding. The courthouse and public square in the center of downtown were decorated with flags and banners, and a large ceremonial arch, seen in this photograph, was constructed on Main Street. Businesses conducted special "centennial sales" and promotional events to appeal to local customers as well as the expected influx of tourists, who would be in the city for the celebration. The centerpiece of the planned events was the centennial parade featuring local marching bands, floats sponsored by civic organizations, churches, schools, and businesses and a variety of marching groups. Some parade entries celebrated the early days of the community, while others demonstrated the latest developments in industry and civic services. The city and citizens collectively celebrated a century of growth and development, solidifying dreams for a century to come.

The Franklin Fire Department entered its modern apparatus in the parade, demonstrating to the citizens that they and their property were being protected by the latest technology in firefighting. Large, devastating fires were an all-too-common event, especially in downtown settings where buildings were literally wall to wall, most with aging wood interior structures often heated with freestanding coal or wood stoves. In prior years, Franklin had suffered the loss of two courthouses and a significant portion of the downtown in such fires. With the potential of fire being a public concern, it was important that cities invest in the best firefighting equipment they could afford, and the elected officials welcomed any opportunity to show the public that they were being diligent in this critical public-safety issue.

The conclusion of World War I was only a few years past at the time of the centennial celebration, and certainly the events and organizations of the war years were still fresh in the memories of all but the youngest residents. Principal among the organizations that were fostered by the war, the Red Cross was highly visible throughout the community. During the war years, much of the Red Cross activity was associated with the military, based at the county fairgrounds, and at Franklin College, but after the war the organization redirected its efforts toward civic services. The Red Cross launched programs to provide disaster and emergency relief for victims of fires, floods, major storms, and other major public incidents. Its presence in the centennial parade provided a forum for the public to express appreciation for the efforts of the organization and its many local volunteers.

The Ku Klux Klan manned a float in the community parade during Franklin's centennial celebration. The Klan was a major power in both state and local politics throughout the 1920s. At the height of its popularity, Johnson County had between 2,000 and 3,000 Klansmen, which equaled nearly 10 percent of the county's adult male population. Klan leader D.C. Stephenson visited Franklin on several occasions to promote the organization at fairground rallies. After rallies, the KKK would usually parade down the streets of downtown Franklin. The presence of Klansmen in full dress, armed and patrolling the streets of Franklin, was a disturbing reality in the 1920s. The KKK was very active in Johnson County politics and the school system and was especially vocal in its opposition to Catholics and nonwhite residents. The Klan's presence in Johnson County was still evident into the 1970s, as the group continued to maintain a post-office box in Greenwood.

Three

Small-Town
Saturday Night

The December 2, 1940, issue of *Life* magazine included a pictorial feature about Saturday night in small-town America, and Franklin, Indiana, was a logical choice. The pictures and text follow a local family at home and play, concluding the chronicle of their adventures at 10:00 p.m., which was closing time in the city.

There are pictures of the Dunn family kitchen, meal preparations in progress, the family eating supper together, and the boys playing on the farm. In town, the family is seen at various stores, visiting the G.C. Murphy variety store and the Kroger grocery store on the north side of the courthouse square to fulfill their weekly shopping needs. While the parents continued exploring the stores, the boys were left on their own to enjoy a cowboy feature, *Pals of the Silver Sage*, at the Artcraft Theatre.

The lead picture from the *Life* magazine series is iconic, with cars parked three-deep, the sidewalks packed with a well-dressed crowd, and the neon glow of the store lights abuzz. Kroger, Swanks, Standard Grocery, and all the stores on the Jefferson Street strip were compared by the magazine to New York's Broadway on a Saturday night. Rob Shilts, executive director of Franklin Heritage, Inc., owns a copy of the *Life* magazine in which the article appears. In the Franklin Chamber of Commerce publication *Franklin Indiana Community Profile*, Shilts was quoted as saying, "The article was called 'A Small Town's Saturday Night,' and this is the dream and vision we keep in our minds for restoring downtown."

Downtown had it all in the 1940s. People went to Franklin for shopping, government matters, restaurants, and church and then stayed for the nightlife and excitement. There was always something new and different happening downtown, whether it was the arrival of the latest retail gadget, the non-FDA-approved medicine man shows on the corner, or the most recent gossip circulating outside the drugstore. Downtown Franklin was the place to be seen.

With a neighborly nod, a friendly smile, and a firm handshake, this is Franklin on a Saturday night.

Life magazine photographer Bernard Hoffman was sent to Franklin to capture images of what a typical Saturday night was like in small-town America. While local legend sets the normal Saturday-night crowd in downtown at around 10,000 people, Hoffman estimated that about 6,000 folks were present during the day and evening of the actual photo shoot. Regardless of the actual number, the image clearly illustrates that the streets and sidewalks were literally covered by a carpet of residents and vehicles, all in town to spend a fall evening shopping and socializing. The diversity in age of the people in the photograph show that the evening was a family event; children, parents, and even grandparents would combine necessary errands and recreation on these weekly excursions. (Photograph by Bernard Hoffman/Time Life Pictures/Getty Images.)

During the week, the downtown business district closed in early evening, and Sunday was everyone's day of rest. But Saturday afternoon and evening were prime time for entertainment at the movie theaters, socializing at the ice cream shop, and family shopping in the downtown retail outlets. In this photograph of the local five-and-dime store, the aisles that normally are more than adequate for the clientele are packed with the Saturday-night shoppers. The signs in the store are promoting "Candy Week," and a display of Halloween costumes suggests a reason for the timing of it. Just as with the crowd on the street, the diversity of the shoppers illustrates the family nature of the evening. (Photograph by Bernard Hoffman/Time Life Pictures/Getty Images.)

Home entertainment in 1940 generally consisted of playing cards or board games with parents and siblings or perhaps an hour of listening to radio broadcasts of music or news, so especially for the youngsters the weekly excursion to downtown was a special event. While Mom and Dad shopped, socialized, and listened to the 4-H band performing on the courthouse steps, these boys were entrusted to see a cowboy movie at the Artcraft Theatre, where an afternoon of entertainment included cartoons, world news, and a feature movie for less than a quarter. In this family, the boys were allowed to wander and explore around town as long as they stayed together and behaved well. They could enjoy Miller-Yarling ice cream cones for 3¢ per scoop, and a pocketful of candy was only a few cents. Occasionally, they would buy popcorn or soda at the movie theater, but usually they would sneak a pocketful of candy into the matinee. The Artcraft Theatre had a strict policy against bringing in any outside food or drink. Although much of the downtown streetscape of 1940 is barely recognizable today, the Artcraft Theatre has been restored by Franklin Heritage, Inc., and still offers a Saturday matinee, including the cartoons and a feature film that is popular among the today's youth (and the parents and grandparents who recall the original version of years past). (Photograph by Bernard Hoffman/Time Life Pictures/Getty Images.)

Four

THE PLACE TO BE

Beyond the storefronts, and only a few blocks from the courthouse square, the Franklin housing market provided accommodations for successful businessmen and lawyers who enjoyed the short and friendly walk to work each day. The ornate homes surrounding the Franklin College campus housed college administrators and professors. Walking the streets of Franklin today, one can see a variety of architectural styles, from magnificent Victorian and antebellum mansions to modest clapboard and shotgun houses. The variety of homes within the community demonstrates a melting pot of class diversity, with unique, century-old restored estates next to homes that meet the modest needs of blue-collar workers.

A healthy downtown residential environment is indicative of a prosperous central business district. In the mid-1900s, the heart of Franklin consisted of a variety of family-owned businesses central to the community's identity. The Arnold family operated the old Franklin Pharmacy, complete with a lunch counter and soda fountain. Nick Banos was frequently found manning his Franklin Candy Kitchen, known by the locals as "Nick's." The Nook, located at State and South Streets, entertained students from Franklin College.

Trueman Rembusch, owner of the Artcraft Theatre, doubled as projectionist, concessionaire, and usher. Ralph Harmon's Double Cola business was doing well, as was the McCarty Bakery, the Ross Floral Company, Joe's Barber Shop, Collins Jewelry, Davis Shoes, and a host of other small-town enterprises. The entrepreneurial spirit was flourishing in Franklin.

Aside from central retail and service businesses, there were many employment opportunities. The county courthouse and city government generated legal and public-service jobs, while Franklin College and the public schools provided education-sector jobs. Other major employers included Noblitt-Sparks (later Arvin Industries), Varynit Mills, Hougland Canning, Morgan Packing, Franklin Pure Milk, the mills, ice and coal facilities, area farms, and residential and health service providers, including the Masonic Home and Methodist Community.

It was a time of competition and changing social and business protocols. Early chain stores discovered the Franklin market, including G.C. Murphy, Kroger, Dog "N" Suds, and Linders Ice Cream, and challenged the mom-and-pop, small-town business climate.

As a testament to the past, this cement boot step hitching post stood near the center of town, well past the days of the horse and buggy. This urban artifact, located at Adams Street and Home Avenue near the busy courthouse square, remained a symbolic reminder of Franklin's longevity as a community.

Cars need gas! Several service stations began to dot the Franklin landscape, and after a lengthy transition, these facilities gradually replaced the old livery businesses. Hunt's Standard Service was family operated and became a popular place to refuel and catch the latest community gossip. As seen in this photograph, the exteriors of these stations often featured advertising for local businesses—in this case, Deer & Son Hardware.

The sheer number of service stations—both in town and on the outskirts—verified the increasing popularity of personal motor vehicles. If a corner did not contain a church or bar, one would likely find a service and fueling facility. Above, a mechanic takes a break at Hunt's Service Station. Below, a classic Gulf service station sits snugly in the shadows of area business. Gulf was noted for marketing slogans that focused on alliteration, including "Good Gulf Gasoline" and "Gulf—the gas with guts." Gulf often built stations in small towns with growth potential and expanded rapidly. Unfortunately, like many of the independent service stations in town, large chain operations eventually laid claim to the Franklin market.

Located east of downtown along Indiana Highway 144, McClain's Service Station was a risky gamble from the start. While most gas stations were in town, many of which providing repair services, McClain's was just a fuel and snack shack. Capturing the traffic from Bargersville to the west, Ira McClain's station began operation in the early 1940s.

Running a service station was often a family affair. One such station just outside Franklin was the C and M Service Station, also known as Coffman Battery Repair. A future "grease monkey," hoping that he will be able to reach the nozzle, stands guard by the old pump awaiting the next customer.

Commissioned by early residents William and Cynthia McCaslin as a family house, this impressive structure was sold in 1922 and later expanded by new owners Eliza Patterson Willard and Mrs. Will Judah to become the Willard Hotel, marketed as the "coziest hotel" in Indiana. The Willard Hotel eventually closed and now operates as a restaurant and bar. At Halloween, the unused portions of the building, including the basement and upper floor, serve as a community haunted house.

By the late 20th century, times were changing in Franklin. Mom-and-pop stores, restaurants, and service businesses were rapidly being replaced by popular franchises and nationwide stores. This is a ribbon-cutting ceremony for a new Applebee's restaurant in 1995. Assisted by local community and company dignitaries, Franklin mayor Charles Littleton is ready to cut the official opening ribbon.

Dr. Harold Richardson (left) and Mayor Jarvis Alexander (right) have a cow-milking contest in support of a Maxwell Street business promotion in 1959. While many Franklin businesses have disappeared since 1959, so has Maxwell Street; it was renamed East Court Street because of the courthouse occupying one side of the street.

In this September 28, 1963, image, Raymond Fuller of the Franklin Chamber of Commerce (left) greets Indiana lieutenant governor Richard Ristine as he visits during Old Fashion Bargain Days in support of downtown business. As early as the 1950s, Franklin leaders were working hard to preserve the business climate around the courthouse square.

Deer's Hardware and Appliances was representative of the hometown businesses that flourished in the downtown area. Local advertising was plentiful, including direct mailings, billboard advertisements, and, most importantly, word of mouth. Small communities supported local and family-owned businesses, but the price advantage of mass retailers made it difficult to compete.

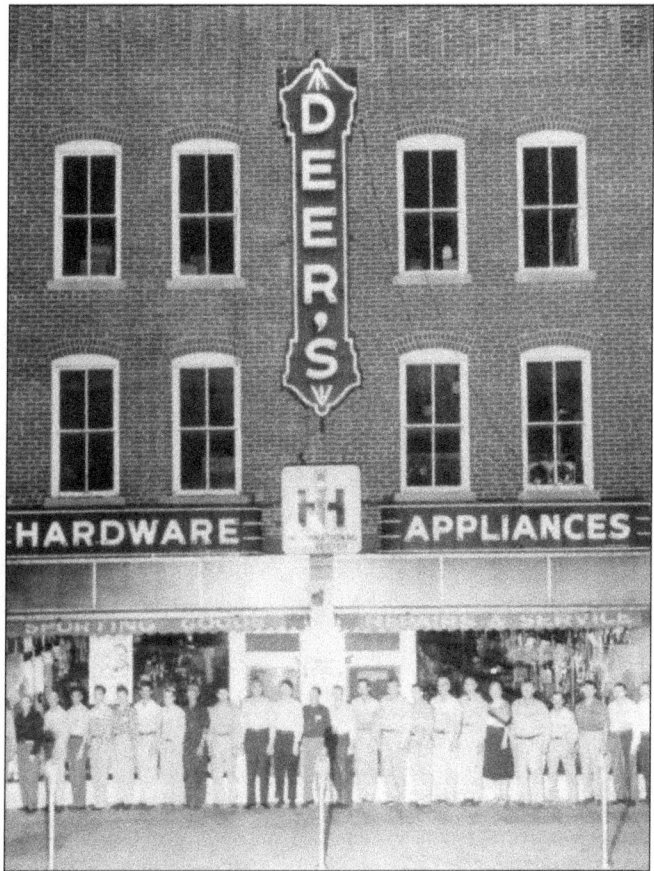

While the Willard Hotel and various boardinghouses served visitors arriving by train and interurban, small motels sprouted up primarily along US Highway 31 to catch the over-the-road travelers; the Sleep-N-Time was one such motel. While the Willard Hotel and downtown boardinghouses closed as car travel increased, the motels along US Highway 31 also began to struggle, as construction of Interstate 65 to the east of town brought a popular interchange and new chain hotels.

The December 21, 1950, Varynit Mills Christmas party is pictured here. Located at 101 East Wayne Street, the facility supplied military uniforms and clothing for soldiers during World War II. After Varynit closed, the building was occupied by a variety of tenants, including Kaygee, noted for producing athletic uniforms (including the team outfits used in the movie *Hoosiers*).

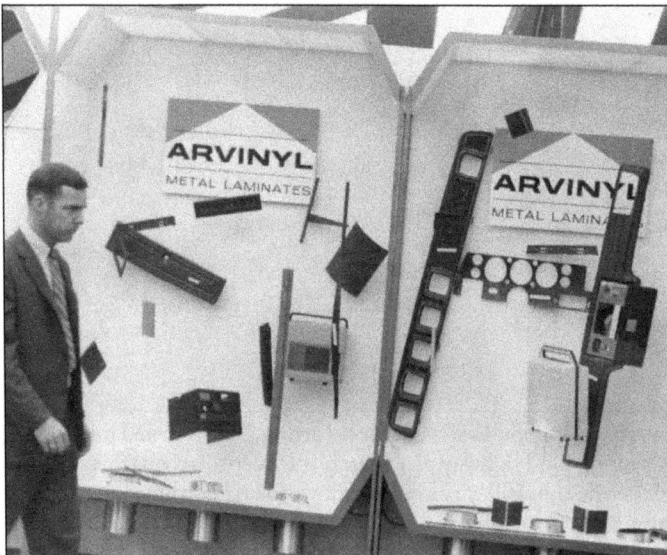

Arvinyl metal laminates are displayed here during the Arvin Industries 50th anniversary celebration. Arvin continually reinvented itself, transitioning from producing mufflers and portable electric heaters to fulfilling government contracts during the 1940s war effort. During Arvin's diverse history, varied metal fabrication included a line of twisted metal lawn chairs and bicycle pumps. It even ventured into television in the 1960s.

Arvin Industries' 50th anniversary logo is proudly displayed by company representatives in this image. With a history dating back to 1919 (as the Indianapolis Air Pump Company), the company became Noblitt-Sparks in 1927. It was 1950 before the company name was finally changed to Arvin Industries to capitalize on the well-known Arvin brand.

This aerial photograph of US Highway 31 north of town shows the development gradually converting agricultural land into business facilities. Now, the same people who enjoyed cruising through town in their spiffy vehicles for leisure cruise the outskirts of town on the way to work. The area surrounding the core business district of Franklin now includes several areas of industrial and commercial development.

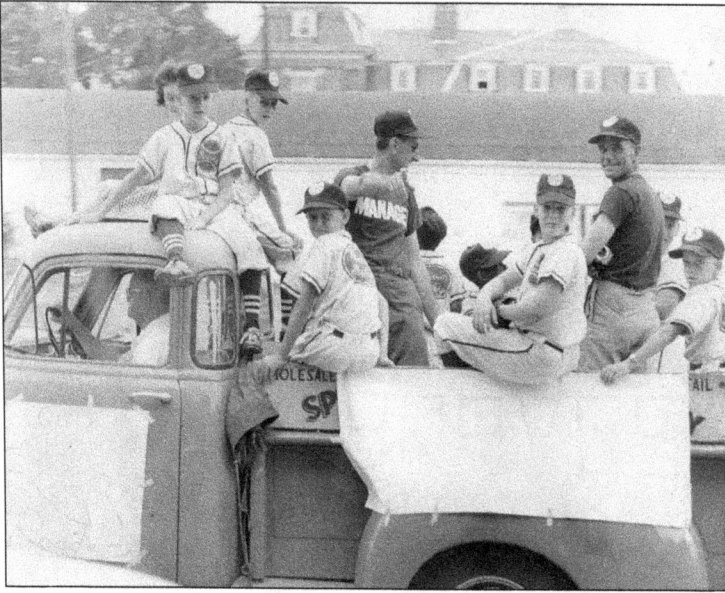

Living in Franklin was not all work. In this 1960 image, Coach Pete is seen driving his Little League team to a big game. Of note in this photograph is the brick jail in the background. Because there was not a jail facility in early Franklin, offenders were locked in rooms in the community and watched. Rumor has it that early prisoners were also bound to trees.

The house located at 200 East Madison Street became the Franklin Girls' Club in 1945. Originally built in 1870 by Henry Vawter, the house had several owners and purposes, including a "Dixie Tearoom." In later years, the building was occupied by the Youth Foundation, whose mission is to serve all young women with a variety of character-building programs.

The Franklin Skate Club, located on the northern outskirts of town, has served the community for years. Many residents have fond memories of learning to skate, school skating parties, and special dates. Aside from skating, the community has supported a variety of bowling facilities, most recently the HiWay Lanes, located farther south on US Highway 31. (Authors' collection.)

Golf has been important in the life of affluent Franklin residents. This 1941 photograph depicts two individuals, identified only as Rags (left) and Jeff, eager to hit the course. In the early days, Hillview Country Club was the Franklin Country Club, which opened in 1926, and was the only golf course in town. Hillview now shares the spotlight with the modern Legends of Indiana Golf Club and the nearby Cypress Run Golf Course.

Hillview Country Club features 6,585 yards of golf from the longest tees for a par of 72. As the oldest and most historic country club facility in Johnson County, continuous upgrades keep the facilities and course fresh. The relatively flat terrain is gentle to walk, and it has a slope rating of 120, which is a bit more difficult than average. Frequent golfers warn novice players about the well-known and very tricky 13th hole.

The Franklin Polo and Saddle Club was a truly unique amenity available to the more affluent members of the Franklin community; few Indiana cities had saddle and polo clubs. The club originally met in various locations, most frequently at the Johnson County Fairgrounds or at members' houses and stables, but later maintained its own clubhouse.

Franklin originally enjoyed classic silent films on the third floor of city hall in a facility known as the Opera House, which ceased operations in 1929. In the following years, both the Artcraft and Franklin Theaters proved popular with area residents. The Artcraft catered more to families with comedies and serials, while the Franklin concentrated on more mature romances and dramas. The Franklin Theater was owned by Syndicated Theaters, which eventually closed the facility; the building was remodeled to house the Mutual Building and Loan. There was also a small theater on Jefferson Street, but little has been written about the facility, and few remember anything about the movie house. As time progressed, the Artcraft survived, but the owners, the Rembusch family, sold the theater due to the changing economics of having just one screen. Canary Creek opened in 2000, providing Franklin with multiple modern screens. The cinema also decided to utilize a parking area south of the cinema as a drive-in movie theater. Since drive-ins are considered a dying proposition, and nationally very few outdoor screens have opened in the last few decades, Canary Creek definitely made headlines. (Authors' collection.)

The historic Johnson County Fairgrounds entrance, shown above, is accessible off North Main Street. A modest track was constructed for horse racing, and in later years, auto dirt-track racing also filled the grandstands. Since the fair did not charge admission, it was difficult to maintain and grow the facility. The building and grounds were rented out for special events; however, the fair's main purpose was not to make money but to encourage and recognize agricultural achievements. At left, Eileen Humes (left) and Jean Davis are all smiles with their winning ribbons. (Above, authors' collection.)

Parades were always welcome affairs in Franklin. In this image from a 1956 parade, James Al is driving Mayor L.W. Oliver in an antique Chevrolet touring car. In recent years, Franklin's major annual parade occurs during the Fall Festival; however, both Franklin College and the Johnson County Fairgrounds sponsor frequent parades. Franklin's best-attended parade of all time remains the 1923 centennial parade.

This photograph depicts a United Service Organization (USO) gathering in the mid-1940s. As a private, nonprofit organization formed to boost morale and provide recreational services to members of the US military, the USO was an active association in Franklin. The USO was founded in 1941 and provided World War II soldiers with entertainment and relaxation.

Preparation for the Thanksgiving meal at the Franklin United Methodist Community includes the teamwork of both professional and volunteer staff. The facility has been known to provide substantial holiday meals to Franklin residents in need. The community has been blessed with tremendous growth, originating in 1957 with the construction of a small apartment complex.

The volunteer spirit has always been an important part of the Franklin community. Here, students perform grounds work at the Franklin United Methodist Community. In the background, the community's large health center is visible. The community has expanded several times since 1957 on its beautiful, sprawling 125-acre campus.

Continuing the volunteer spirit, this group of Boy Scouts collects items for its annual food drive. Despite Franklin's overall prosperity, the community has a fair share of residents below Indiana's poverty level. The annual Boy Scout food drive was well supported by area residents and businesses, with over 100 care baskets usually distributed.

What happens when a neighbor experiences a disaster? The community comes together to assist those in need. This large volunteer group is working to restore a home destroyed by fire. From severe flooding to large-scale fires and other natural disasters, the Franklin community is known to take care of its citizens.

Fires can be devastating events, and Franklin College has experienced several fires throughout its history. Bryan Hall is pictured here in 1985 before (above) and after (below) a major fire. Because many students were left without beds and personal belongings were lost to flames, temporary shelter was provided by the college. The Franklin community was also empathetic to the students' situation and offered to house students in private residences. When the town has been affected by flood, fire, or tornado, numerous recorded examples display the heart of Franklin.

This iconic Benjamin Franklin statue is one of the most active landmarks in the city. Numerous times during the school year, this Franklin College fixture becomes a conduit of student creativity. Students decorate Franklin to communicate holiday greetings, as well as political messages and timely social commentary. "Ben" frequently sports a new coat of paint.

Two students enjoy the M.A. and Paul Branigin Franklin College fishpond. Rumor has it that the pond possesses special magic, and students often use the pond as a wishing well. While the Franklin College campus is blessed with natural beauty, recent years have seen major beautification efforts, including a new campus entrance.

Opening in 1947 on land just west of the city, Johnson Memorial Hospital has grown with the city. The hospital began as a memorial to the men and women from Johnson County who served in World War II, but it has expanded to include a bariatric care center, an acute rehabilitation center, an occupational health specialty area, and, in 2005, a state-of-the-art cancer care center. (Authors' collection.)

Containing over 15,000 graves, Greenlawn Cemetery occupies 40 acres at 100 West South Street. The cemetery is the final resting place for over 700 military veterans. It is also a hot spot for paranormal researchers. Numerous unexplained incidents have reportedly occurred in the cemetery, including ghost sightings; some interesting images have been captured through spiritual photography. (Authors' collection.)

Spring is a magical time in the city. The trees come alive and flowers bloom from the mature landscapes—as do the blossoms of romance. Here, a multitude of attendees enjoy themselves at Franklin College's spring formal, dubbed "Maytime." Franklin College hosts many dances, both formal and informal, during the academic year.

This photograph shows the highly recognizable and charming Franklin Chamber of Commerce office, located next to the East Jefferson Street tracks. Originally the New York Central Railroad Depot, known as the Big Four Stop, the building has also housed the office of the Johnson County United Way, Red Cross, and the Educational Foundation. This building also houses a small railroad museum. (Authors' collection.)

This train car is a permanent fixture in front of the relocated train depot. Originally located in Martin Place on Water Street, the depot was moved to its present location at 370 East Jefferson Street in 1990. The restoration and relocation project was funded by the Franklin Chamber of Commerce and the Johnson County Educational Foundation. (Authors' collection.)

With a corner station at the intersection of South Main and South Streets, the Franklin Police Department had a highly visible location. The unique building once housed a Mobile gas station and a restaurant. At one time, Franklin had a red globe call box on East Jefferson Street used for quickly contacting the police.

The Johnson County Courthouse Annex was a needed addition to downtown. As the county's population swelled, especially with the influx of people to Greenwood in the north, there was just not room within the existing courthouse to adequately serve county residents. Built in 1982, this structure houses numerous county offices.

It is interesting to see a public official creating a little graffiti; a Franklin firefighter helps deliver the message that Fire Prevention Week activities are about to begin. With so many older homes and buildings within the city and few originally outfitted with electricity, numerous structures were prone to fires.

In this image, Franklin mayor Frank Records and his wife, Eunice, greet Mrs. America 1961, Rosemary Murphy. Franklin has hosted a variety of famous people and entertainers over the years. Franklin College has been known to feature an assortment of national speakers, effectively bringing the world to the city.

As the seat of Johnson County government, Franklin has welcomed many important national and state political leaders. In this 1970 image, popular Democrat Birch Bayh (left) takes time to pose for a photograph during a campaign visit. A long-gone Texaco service station and the landmark Johnson County Courthouse are visible in the background.

These two beautiful and recent postcards were made available by the Franklin Chamber of Commerce. Captured above is an atmospheric courthouse image complete with a rainbow. The postcard below contains four images: the familiar and modern "Welcome to Franklin" sign, an elevated view of downtown Franklin, and two courthouse shots. It cannot be argued that Franklin's most distinctive architectural treasure is the courthouse. Two other significant landmark structures include the August Zeppenfeld House, built in 1872 and located at 300 West Jefferson Street, an Italianate architectural jewel listed on the National Register of Historic Places, and the Masonic Temple, home of the Johnson County Historical Society and Museum of History, built in 1924 and reflective of the Classical architectural style. (Franklin Chamber of Commerce.)

Near completion of construction on the fifth and current courthouse, these unidentified workers take a break during installation of the cupola. Construction commenced in 1879, but the courthouse did not open to the public until 1882; in the meantime, a temporary structure was built to conduct court business. The modillions, columns, pilasters, and pediments on the courthouse highlight strong and varied ornamentation borrowed from Beaux-Arts and Neoclassical styles. The limestone and brick offer a brilliant contrast highlighting the horizontals. While the clock tower is visible around town, there are also four corner towers, known as a Harrisonburg Plan, keeping vigil over the community. Designed by prolific Indiana courthouse architect George W. Bunting, his creation followed four previous courthouses. The fourth courthouse, a magnificent structure designed by Edwin May, who also designed the Indiana Statehouse, fell to flames in 1874.

Five

POSTCARD VIEWS

When people think of New York City, they may envision the Statue of Liberty, Central Park, the Empire State Building, and Times Square. When Indianapolis comes to mind, it possibly inspires thoughts about the Indianapolis Motor Speedway, Monument Circle, or maybe a favorite restaurant. Those who live, or have lived, in Franklin might remember the Artcraft Theatre, a specific building on the Franklin College campus, visiting the Indiana Masonic Home, or even a special event or parade. While people define a community, it is the physical space itself—the houses, businesses, parks, and events—that helps to define the people. It is said that a man is judged by where and how he spends his life.

Postcards are able to capture a snapshot in time, one that may only have existed in the mind's eye, because people often do not take the time to preserve the memories of their lives. Joe Seiter, one of the founding members and a past president of the Indianapolis Postcard Club, has said when looking through a stack of old postcards, "If it weren't for these postcards, we wouldn't have a clue. In many instances, a postcard is the only visible evidence of places and things in our past." The authors know from current and previous research efforts that Joe's words ring true.

Franklin is blessed with a variety of postcards produced throughout the city's history. Images include major streets, businesses, transportation, events, public and private buildings, and various natural scenes. The number and quality of postcard images rival those of much larger cities.

Used postcards sent through the mail often contain messages on the back that reveal unknown information through first-person reporting. If sent through the mail, a postmark will give the researcher an idea about when the illustration was rendered or photograph taken. Unfortunately, fewer and fewer postcards are being produced in these digital times. The next several pages include postcard images of Franklin's past.

South Entrance to Johnson County Court House, Franklin, Ind.

The most iconic symbol of Franklin is the Johnson County Courthouse. Seen in this postcard about 1900, only a few years after completion, the imposing structure dominates the landscape of the public square. If, as sociologists believe, importance in the life of a community is reflected by location, the courthouse is certainly the most important structure in town.

JOHNSON COUNTY COURT HOUSE, FRANKLIN, INDIANA   N-349

This view of the courthouse, now 60 years old, shows the growth of the downtown area. Many of the buildings that now surround the public square house the lawyers, bankers, and merchants who were drawn to the center of the town by the presence of the courthouse. The singular imposing structure, now surrounded by its progeny, still marks the center of social life in Franklin.

West on Jefferson from Water St., Franklin, Ind.

Jefferson Street, bordering the north side of the public square, is the major commercial thoroughfare through downtown. In these postcard images looking west (above) and east (below) from the center of the business district, one can see early commercial buildings before the popularization of the automobile. The streets are mostly occupied by pedestrian traffic, with only a few vehicles visible. Above, an automobile has the street all to itself. The first recorded automobile in Franklin was a 1901 Oldsmobile owned by a local businessman who reportedly drove it through downtown occasionally, gathering notable attention with each trip.

EAST JEFFERSON STREET, FRANKLIN, IND

I. O. O. F. Building, Franklin, Ind.

These two postcards illustrate the dramatic changes in the downtown business district in the first 20 years of the 1900s. In the view above, the formerly quiet street is now crowded with cars, some even double-parked, as shoppers take advantage of a "dissolution sale" at a local retail store. In the foreground is a service station located in the center of the business district, a sign that the days of the horse and buggy are gone and the mechanical revolution is firmly in place. The view at left shows the gradual change in the appearances of the buildings themselves as retailers modernized, adding canvas awnings and large display windows to attract pedestrian traffic.

East Madison Street, Franklin, Ind.

The arrival of electric railroad service in the early 1900s made travel to downtown—and even other towns and cities—a practical reality. As seen in these postcard views, the tracks were located in the center of the street, and the train was powered by overhead wires. Passengers could board and disembark at stops located at intervals along the route. In the view above, a group of passengers awaits the trolley along East Madison Street. Note the sign on the utility pole denoting a stop on the route. The view below illustrates the obstacle to cars or carriages posed by the rails down the center of Main Street; carriages and early cars had narrow wheels that were ill suited for crossing the protruding rails, and drivers had to be cautious to avoid getting stuck on the tracks.

North Main St. looking North from St. Car Station, Franklin, Ind.

Partial View of the Plant of Valentine & Valentine at Franklin, Indiana.
Elevator Capacity 135,000 bushels. Feed Warehouse Capacity 600 tons.

This postcard view from the dawn of the 20th century focuses primarily on the imposing plant of Valentine and Valentine, a long-established mill that provided grain, feed, and similar agricultural supplies, along with grain elevator and storage facilities. A major portion of the feed business was supplying the numerous livery stables in and near the town. The principal mode of transportation at this time is shown in the numerous horse-drawn wagons around the loading docks—but nestled among the wagons is a single automobile, a sign of things to come. Within a generation, the automobile, and the trucks that would join it, would forever change the nature of this business and others like it. While motorized tractors and trucks improved farming and increased the business for grain elevators and storage facilities, they virtually eliminated much of the feed business that depended on supplying livery stables.

While Franklin was conceived and established as the seat of Johnson County government, the city also had its own operations to manage. The first city hall (above) was built in 1895. This three-story structure, located just south of the public square, provided a central location for all city offices. The building also had space for public meetings, and part of the space was used as an opera house for several years. The center of the city soon proved to be an impractical location for many city functions, so a new building (below) was constructed to house the operations.

CITY BUILDING, FRANKLIN, INDIANA   N-350

During the post–World War II period, the US Post Office embarked on a program of building hundreds of new post offices across the nation. In Franklin, the new building seen here replaced the former post office located in a downtown storefront. The postal service used a standardized design for the expansion program, so the building seen here is typical of those found in medium-sized cities nationwide.

As was the case in any thriving city, the community outgrew its school buildings. This early-1900s view is of the "new" Franklin High School, which provided more classroom space and offices for the rapidly expanding student population. Franklin High School has long been known for its excellent academic and sports programs.

First Ward Grade School, Franklin, Ind.

Education is and always has been a central value in Franklin. The earliest schools were small one-room facilities, but as the population grew, the city began to construct proper public schools. By the dawn of the 20th century, the city was investing heavily in first-class educational facilities. These two postcard views illustrate the size and quality of construction of the elementary schools, certainly state of the art for the time. The fact that people made postcards showing these schools illustrates the local pride in the school system, since townspeople could mail them to acquaintances as examples of the city's features.

Central Grade School Building, Franklin, Ind.

Franklin College, Franklin, Ind.

Pub by S C Yager

Higher education also found a home in Franklin. Established in 1834, when the town was just 10 years old, Franklin College occupies a large campus on the east side of the city. Originally established by a group of American Baptists as a seminary, the college led Indiana in offering coeducational programming. The school closed briefly during the Civil War but reopened and began an aggressive building program. Pictured above is the building known as Old Main, the first significant step in the expansion and revitalization of the college. Below is an image of the early campus, much of which is now occupied by educational and student residence buildings.

College Campus, Franklin, Ind.

GYMNASIUM

As Franklin College grew and prospered, numerous new buildings were erected on the campus. Construction projects ranged from the utilitarian gymnasium (above) to the spectacular residence erected by Professor Bryan (below). Although the college is relatively small and located in a small city, the campus and surrounding residential area are filled with architectural masterpieces. The college's newest structures are thoroughly modern, but the school has taken care to preserve and restore many of the older structures, creating a campus that celebrates its historical roots while embracing the present and future.

Prof. Bryan's Residence, Franklin, Ind.

West Madison St., Franklin, Ind.

Franklin's residential neighborhoods generally reflect the typical Middle American culture, as seen in the view of Madison Street shown above. Much of the housing stock in the city was constructed between 1890 and 1940 and is of the craftsman or bungalow style, featuring wood siding with brick porches. However, as the view below illustrates, a number of much more elaborate homes, such as the one in the left foreground, reflect the draw of the county seat to a wealthier, professional population. Also shown in the background below are two substantial churches, typical fixtures in the neighborhoods throughout the city.

Another fixture of Middle America is the locally owned motel. The growth of travel by automobile in the 1950s spawned an entire industry that served the needs of families vacationing or traveling by car to visit friends and family. The change from travel by public transportation, such as rail and bus lines with stations typically located in town centers, brought an end to traditional downtown hotels. A new type of accommodation for travelers—the motel—was born, often with facilities located on the edges of town near principal highways. Franklin's Lake Motel, shown here, was an example of these new operations. Motels offered low-cost sleeping accommodations and plenty of free parking and boasted of free television, air-conditioning, and similar amenities, as well as easy highway access. The later construction of interstate highways that bypass most towns and cities led to the clustering of national chain motels at the various interchanges, leaving these small motels isolated from the principal traffic and causing most of them to close.

Arches, Jefferson St. over
Hurricane Creek, Franklin, Ind.

Postcards are as varied as the interests of photographers and the general audience they hope to entice to purchase their product. This image may have been intended to show the stone bridge or illustrate a serene place offering a respite within the otherwise busy city. In a time when most communication was by mail, people used postcards as a simple way to show a friend or family member a place they had been, highlights of a vacation spot, or a family visit. Many postcards were specifically advertising pieces for a store or product or promoted a place to see or visit. The cards offered limited space for writing but were inexpensive to mail, so the notes were always brief. Modern means of rapid and inexpensive communication have generally replaced the postcard with a telephone call or an e-mail message that serves the same purpose, but, sadly, those will never replace the lasting image of a moment in time provided by postcards.

Six

THE FUTURE OF THE PAST

Franklin Heritage, Inc., was formed in 1983 by a small group of citizens dedicated to the preservation and restoration of Franklin's historic and architectural heritage as an integral part of the community. Its early beginnings focused on establishing a tree-planting program that garnered the City of Franklin the title of Tree City USA for three consecutive years. The group also initiated a program to preserve the brick streets wherever practical. Franklin Heritage has conducted historic home seminars to assist interested citizens in researching the history of older homes, learning about original paint schemes, and performing restoration projects. In 1987, the now-annual historic home tour was inaugurated, promoting education and awareness of historic homes in Franklin.

Franklin Heritage acquired its first property in October 1998. Abandoned for two years, the home at 549 Water Street had become a neighborhood eyesore, was condemned by the city, and was a general dumping place for all manner of trash and debris. Over the course of a year, Franklin Heritage was able to restore the property and sell it for a small profit, generating seed money for the next property.

Over the past decade, Franklin Heritage has completed a total of 10 historic restoration projects. Eight homes have been restored, along with the Artcraft Theatre and the building that now houses the Franklin Heritage offices. In each instance, the restored property has become a catalyst for additional development, renovation, and investment. To date, Franklin Heritage has invested over $1 million in the Franklin community through these restoration projects.

In the same way that the unique characteristics of historic homes set them apart from new construction and add value to the structure, the restoration of such homes adds value to the community. Each of the homes that Franklin Heritage has restored and resold has resulted in significant increases in property values and encouraged nearby homeowners to improve their own properties. Unmeasured in dollars is the value of added neighborhood stability and the sense of pride and unity that is engendered by neighborhood improvements.

—Rob Shilts
Executive Director, Franklin Heritage, Inc.

The Artcraft Theatre, seen above in 1940 and below as it looks today, was, is, and always will be an old friend to the Franklin community. Changing economics made a one-screen theater with a massive auditorium difficult to maintain, let alone to turn a profit. Owner Mike Rembusch recognized the impossibilities of the situation and sold the Artcraft in May 2000. Purchased by Bob and Mike Schofield shortly after closing, Franklin Heritage began the "Classic Cinema on a Classic Screen" series to support the theatre; the series was a success, and Franklin Heritage bought the facility in 2004 for $175,000. Franklin Heritage continues to heavily invest in the restoration of the theatre and show old movies on the screen, complete with a live skit, the national anthem, and a cartoon preceding the feature film. (Franklin Heritage, Inc.)

After being involved in more 911 calls than any other house in Franklin, local police were glad to see the rescue of the house pictured above. At the house, located on the edge of the Franklin College campus, restoration workers encountered dangerous debris, including numerous exposed needles and assorted drug paraphernalia. The house had been divided into four apartments, and a crudely installed security camera mounted at the back door provided additional clues about the activities of recent occupants. Inside, the original staircase, with the top half removed, had been boarded over, and an outside staircase allowed entrance to the upstairs apartments. Known as the 1890 Carpenter-Builder home, the house located at 901 East Jefferson Street was refurbished (below) and resold in 2008, just over a year from the date of acquisition. (Franklin Heritage, Inc.)

The 1895 Queen Anne–style home seen above had been vacant for 27 years, and the house was in danger of demolition. Upon acquisition by Franklin Heritage, it was discovered that the home contained many of the original contents, including a recliner resting in front of a 1960s television set and dirty dishes still stacked in the kitchen sink. Photographs on the walls depicted happier times at the property. Franklin Heritage began acquisition and restoration of the house, located at 425 East Jefferson Street, in May 2005. The home contained an original kitchen, two unaltered bathrooms, three sets of French doors, and an elegant built-in china cabinet. An open house prior to restoration brought a crowd of 400 people to see the tarnished gem, including two newspapers and a television station. The restored house is pictured below. (Franklin Heritage, Inc.)

This 1870 home with classic Italianate architecture sat vacant for 11 years. The home's original, beautiful "fish-scale" shingles had been covered with low-quality aluminum siding (above). Inside the house, a magnificent curved wooden staircase, an impressive fireplace and mantel, and other unique features were still present; however, the house at 248 North Water Street was an eyesore. The restored home (below) was a featured stop on Franklin Heritage's 2006 Historic Home Tour. The vibrant, original colors hidden by the siding were restored, and the decorative brackets supporting the overhanging eaves were returned to their original splendor. The wraparound porch, one of the most architecturally pleasing porches in town, was ready to receive guests once again. Franklin Heritage continues restoration projects in Franklin, offering an investment in the past and ensuring a promising future. (Franklin Heritage, Inc.)

These two photographs—a historic home located at 2 Morton Place (above) and the Red Men's Building at 354 East Morton Place (below)—depict two significant, well-maintained properties in Franklin. Other properties have not fared as well. Aside from the examples detailed within these pages, Franklin Heritage has saved additional properties in Franklin, including 800 East King Street, 549 Hurricane Street, 600 Hurricane Street, and 49 East Madison Street. The City of Franklin, along with Franklin Heritage, advocates for a healthy downtown area. While other cities consider, or have considered, razing significant buildings in their downtown business districts, Franklin continues to invest heavily in historic preservation.

Greetings from Franklin, Ind.

Every town of considerable size seems to have circulated a "greetings from" postcard. While the image is probably not unique to Franklin, it does embody the agricultural roots of the community. The apparently hardworking men are looking at the camera and seem to be friendly chaps. The bottom detail reads, "Greetings from Franklin, Ind." In contrast, today's Franklin, while retaining its agricultural core, is a diverse city with a growing population. The franchised stores along US Highway 31 neighbor the downtown core, but the central area remains the heart and soul of the community. Ever proud, the city maintains a unique identity and is not much bothered by Indianapolis to the north, successfully avoiding any "bedroom community" moniker. The city is professional and calculating, yet down-to-earth and accessible. There is pride in the courthouse, charming downtown, successful businesses and factories, well-reputed liberal arts college, world-class hospital, and so much more. Franklin is a place where history meets future, where the true essence of community can unintentionally be found in old Norman Rockwell paintings. Franklin is home!

Visit us at
arcadiapublishing.com